Key capabilities in
Child Care
and protection

ISBN: 0-7559-5235-9

Scottish Executive
St Andrew's House
Edinburgh
EH1 3DG

Produced for the Scottish Executive by Astron B48491 12/06

Published by the Scottish Executive, December, 2006

Further copies are available from
Blackwell's Bookshop
53 South Bridge
Edinburgh
EH1 1YS

The text pages of this document are printed on recycled paper and are 100% recyclable

Ministerial Foreword

Social workers have a key role in protecting our most vulnerable children. It is vital that the honours degree in social work properly equips them with the knowledge, skills and understanding they need to deal with child care and child protection issues. Whilst individual social workers and employers have responsibilities for continuing professional development beyond the initial qualification, it is crucial that the degree should provide a solid foundation on which deeper knowledge and skills can be built.

The Key Capabilities in Child Care and Protection provide an important step forward. These are learning outcomes and competencies in relation to child care and protection in social work degree programmes and have been developed by the Scottish Institute for Excellence in Social Work Education in consultation with key stakeholders. They enhance and are aligned to the more generic *Standards in Social Work Education* (SiSWE) as laid out in the *Framework for Social Work Education in Scotland*[1].

It is now vital for those concerned with social work education in Scotland, including universities and employers, to work in partnership to embed the Key Capabilities in the degree programmes. Only through doing this can a consistent approach be achieved which will produce better outcomes for service users.

The Scottish Executive is committed to its vision for children which says that they need to be safe, nurtured, healthy, achieving, active, respected, responsible and included. We are also committed to achieving a competent and confident social work workforce equipped to make this vision a reality. The provision of high quality social work education is a fundamental cornerstone in this process and I am convinced the Key Capabilities will provide an excellent framework for new social workers to make their own contribution. With your help, we can ensure that they are given the best preparation to provide the level of care and protection our most vulnerable children deserve.

[1] http://www.scotland.gov.uk/Publications/2003/01/16202/17015

Executive Summary

The Key Capabilities (KCs) in Child Care and Protection are designed to allow students within social work degree programmes to map their specific learning in this area whilst achieving the more generic Standards in Social Work Education (SiSWE). The KCs further allow social work students to evidence their learning in child care and protection by their progress being assessed at the mid and end points of the programme. Key Capabilities are essentially the key areas of learning that students should be capable of achieving in relation to child care and protection both during and by the end of their social work degree programme.

The Key Capabilities document has four headings which together form the KCs in Child Care and Protection:

1. Effective Communication;
2. Knowledge and Understanding;
3. Professional Confidence and Competence;
4. Values and Ethical Practice.

Within the document, a set of examples, drawn from experienced university staff and practitioners from the field of child care and protection, recommend how students might evidence their learning at different Scottish Credit and Qualifications Framework (SCQF) levels across a programme under each of these headings.

The KCs are not a new set of standards but rather a mechanism for students and social work programmes to evidence the level of knowledge and understanding that qualified social workers will have achieved at graduation. The KCs are designed to allow all programmes to track their own unique ways of teaching and supporting student learning in the field of child care and protection and be in a position to evidence this through quality assurance processes.

Within this document KCs have been separately aligned to undergraduate and post-graduate social work courses, the first being in relation to undergraduate courses.

Key Capabilities

Throughout this document the term 'child protection' is used in its broadest sense. Different practitioners may have different definitions of what the term child protection represents. Therefore, this should be taken to mean child protection in the context of *child care and meeting children's needs, rather than solely the investigative interviewing process*.

The purpose of Key Capabilities is to ensure that all social workers at the point of qualifying are aware of their roles and responsibilities in respect of children and young people. They are also to ensure that qualifying social workers are able to demonstrate their knowledge, skills and understanding in relation to child care and protection. *Meeting all the Key Capabilities does not qualify emerging social workers to undertake child protection investigations.* This is rightly the domain of post qualifying, continuing professional development, the responsibility being shared by employers and qualified workers. Rather, should they need to engage with a child in the course of their practice, meeting the Key Capabilities should ensure that they are prepared with the skills to do so.

The Key Capabilities are designed for all students. This is based on the assumption that although all qualified practitioners may not be involved in child protection investigative interviews and will not be based within children and families teams, they will all have a generic responsibility towards children and are accountable for their individual actions. All students emerging from universities should have core knowledge, understanding and skills in relation to child care and protection that they can draw on whether they work in adult mental health, criminal justice or other settings. As the title of the Child Protection Audit notes – "It's Everyone's Job to Make Sure I'm Alright" (2002).

Ensuring that students emerge with appropriate skills, knowledge and understanding in relation to child care and protection does not mean that employers' responsibilities for their continuing professional development are reduced. The Scottish Social Services Council (SSSC) Codes of Practice state that employers must provide "induction, training and development opportunities to help social service workers do their jobs effectively and prepare for new and changing roles and responsibilities" (2003, 3.1). In order to develop confident and competent social workers, employers have a responsibility to build on the skills, knowledge and understanding developed prior to qualifying, by providing appropriate supervision and ongoing training opportunities. For example, communicating with children is a complex area that will require further development for some practitioners post-graduation.

Qualified social workers have a responsibility to identify continuing professional development needs, eg newly qualified social workers are required to complete 24 days (144 hours) of Post Registration Training and Learning (PRTL) within 12 months of registration. At least 5 days (30 hours) must focus on working effectively with colleagues and other professionals to identify, assess and manage risk to vulnerable people (SSSC, 2003). In evidencing that they have met the Key Capabilities, students will be starting to take some of the responsibility for their own learning needs, a process which will continue after qualification.

The KCs encourage critical thinking amongst students. Reder and Duncan state that a key aim of training is to "arm practitioners with knowledge, skills and the capacity to think" (2004). It is these principles that underpin all the Key Capabilities but have particular relevance to Professional Competence and Confidence.

The Key Capabilities will define learning outcomes and competencies in relation to child care and protection. The KCs have been mapped with SiSWE and SCQ Frameworks. Account has also been taken of the SSSC Codes of Practice (2003), SE Framework for Standards and Children's Charter (2004), DFES Common Core of Knowledge and Skills for the Children's Workforce (England 2005) and the DoH Requirements for Social Work Training (2002).

Recommendations on approaches to assessment of Key Capabilities and how they can be embedded in practice learning have been made within this document.

Running through all Key Capabilities is an expectation that students will be asked to demonstrate anti oppressive/anti discriminatory practice both in academic and practice learning settings. It is expected that a student's practice will embody the SSSC Codes of Practice which states that they should "promote equal opportunities" and "respect diversity and different cultures and values" (2003, 1.5,1.6). This is set out in the Standards and Audit for Practice Learning Opportunities: A Quality Process (2006). Similarly, it is expected that Higher Education Institutions (HEIs) and Local Authority/Voluntary agencies offering practice learning opportunities will be working within current legislative frameworks to promote equal opportunities for students.

In addition, there is also an expectation that students will access up-to-date research and literature at all stages of their academic career as this should always underpin practice. The use of relevant research and the links students make between theory and practice is an area students would, within the SiSWE, be assessed on by tutors and practice teachers.

The skills of an emerging social work practitioner will change over the course of their training, therefore the way skills are taught and assessed will be incremental and correlate with the relevant stage of learning in accordance with SCQF levels.

Throughout the text core documents and theories have been identified for students to draw from. These documents will change over time to reflect new research, new literature, and unfortunately new Inquiry Reports. As such, the Bibliography which is appended is not set in stone, and it is the responsibility of universities and students to ensure that they remain responsive to change.

Assessment

The assessment of Key Capabilities is based on the premise that all students need to demonstrate core knowledge, understanding and skills in child care and protection to enable them to progress in their studies/practice.

Every student qualifying as a social worker will be assessed in relation to child care and protection at key stages of their learning. **At a minimum, students should undergo summative assessment prior to their first practice learning opportunity and prior to completing the course.**

Dependent on when they have their practice learning opportunity, students may first be assessed at level 8 or 9 (SCQF), however all students should be assessed at level 10 (SCQF) prior to completion. If students do not meet the required level of competence, then they should not progress to the next stage, until such time as they have met that level. For some students this will mean that they cannot undertake their practice learning opportunities at the same time as their peers.

Assessment of Key Capabilities does not preclude assessment of other areas; rather it should be one component of assessing the overall skills of the student.

The responsibility for assessment is a shared one between the student, the tutor, the practice teacher and others including service users and carers.

The student needs to demonstrate that s/he has met the Key Capabilities. They can demonstrate this in formal assessments such as exams and assignments. They can also evidence Key Capabilities through less formal methods of assessment for example, their use of learning logs, their contribution to tutorials, group work, etc.

HEIs can assess students progress and readiness to practice in relation to Key Capabilities using a range of formative and summative assessment methods.

Practice Learning Opportunities

A requirement of the Key Capabilities is that **whatever practice learning opportunity a student is engaged in, they must be able to evidence their knowledge and application of child care and protection, as it is relevant to their setting**. For example, students working in an adult setting might be working with adults who are grandparents, who have regular contact with children, who have caring responsibilities or who have committed sexual offences. Adults have been children and their current difficulties could be connected to experiences from their childhood. Students need to demonstrate that they can make relevant links between child care and protection and their current practice learning opportunity.

A further requirement is that during one of their assessed practice learning opportunities, students should undertake an assessment of a child or of parenting capacity. The student may not necessarily be primary case holder, rather they might be co-working within or across organisations.

Throughout the document there are examples of how a student's learning in child care and protection could be measured. These suggestions are not comprehensive and each HEI and practice teacher may have different methods of assessing a student's learning.

Key Capabilities
aligned with SCQF and SiSWE

KEY CAPABILITIES ALIGNED WITH SCQF AND SiSWE

Effective Communication

Effective communication is intrinsic to all social work practice. In order to be a capable practitioner, students will be required to be effective using a range of methods, in a variety of settings and with different individuals and groups.

The following provides an example of opportunities for students to learn and be assessed on their communication skills in the area of child care and protection.

The following grids should be read in conjunction with the full SCQF and SiSWE documents as components of these have at times been abbreviated.

		SCQF	Standards in Social Work Education
Level 7 **Aim:** **Developing basic communication skills and awareness of particular aspects of communication with children.**	Skills at this level may well be taught within a generic context. However there should be some exploration of age groups and acknowledgement that different skills are required to communicate with children. As Anne Graffam Walker notes "The bottom line in communicating accurately with children is that adults must realise that they and children do not speak the same language" (Forensic Linguist, taken from conference material, Dundee University, 2005).	*Knowledge* - A broad knowledge of the subject.	Preparing for social work contact and involvement: - Understanding the importance of inter-personal factors in delivering effective social work services.
	At this stage students need to receive input and demonstrate some skills in: • Active Listening • The ability to record and summarise information clearly. • The importance of different forms of communication (verbal/non verbal) to their practice.	*Practice* - Use some of the basic and routine professional skills, etc. *Cognitive* - Present and evaluate arguments, information and ideas.	Working with individuals, families etc so that they can make informed decisions: - Listen actively to others; respond appropriately to their life experiences.
	Students need to understand the importance of engaging with people, and forming and maintaining working relationships based on honesty and partnership. The ability to convey information effectively is noted in the SSSC Codes of Practice (2003, 2.2) which states that social workers should communicate in an "appropriate, open, accurate and straightforward way".	*Knowledge* - Knowledge that is embedded in the main theories, concepts and principles. *Communication* - use a range of forms of communication effectively in both familiar and new contexts. *Autonomy* - Take account of own and others' roles and responsibilities in carrying out and evaluating tasks.	Preparing for social work contact: - Make effective contact with individuals and organisations.

		SCQF	Standards in Social Work Education
Level 8 **Aim:** **Opportunities to start practising skills and demonstrating knowledge.**	Students need to be given opportunities to apply their communication skills - within group settings and practice learning opportunities.	*Practice* - Use a range of routine skills, techniques, practices, a few of which are advanced or complex.	Preparing for social work involvement: - Make effective contact with individuals and organisations.
	The Children's Charter and the Framework for Standards (Scottish Executive, both 2004) highlight the importance of listening to children. Standard 3 of the Framework for Standards states that "Professionals ensure that children are listened to and respected".	*Autonomy* - Deal with ethical and professional issues in accordance with current professional and/or ethical codes of practice.	Working with individuals etc so they can make informed decisions: - Explain and negotiate the purpose of contacts and the boundaries of their involvement.
	In preparation for practice learning opportunities: Students need to demonstrate knowledge and skills in communicating where English is not the first language or where the primary form of communication is non- verbal. For example, students should be aware of their legal responsibilities to access interpreter services and know how to do this and their responsibility to use relevant specialist services to enable them to listen and communicate with children who use alternative forms of communication (for example signing).	*Practice* - Adapt routine practices within accepted standards.	Working with groups to promote choice: - Identify and use opportunities for purposeful and supportive communication. Understanding and managing complex ethical issues: - Knowledge of equal opportunities and anti-discriminatory legislation and practice.
	Students need to be able to show that they can build on their understanding of how children communicate. For example, when a child displays proximity seeking behaviour such as pulling on one's sleeve, they are trying to attract attention and have their needs met. Students need to demonstrate that they are observing children's behaviour and starting to consider what this non-verbal communication might tell them about children's experiences.	*Knowledge* - understanding of a limited range of core theories, principles and concepts. *Cognitive* - undertake critical analysis, evaluation and/or synthesis of ideas.	Tackling behaviour which presents a risk: - Use both verbal and non-verbal cues to guide interpretations of behaviour and assess risk.
	Students will have the opportunity to practise conveying complex information in a group setting. For example, alongside students from other disciplines within the HEI (e.g. health/education) they could role play a case conference. This includes written and verbal presentation of information.	*Communication* - Convey complex information to a range of audiences and for a range of purposes.	Preparing for and taking part in decision making forums: - Communicate clearly, accurately and precisely with individuals and groups in a range of formal and informal situations.

		SCQF	Standards in Social Work Education
Level 9 **Aim:** **Ability to demonstrate and use a selection of skills in contexts which include a degree of unpredictability.**	Students should be able to communicate directly with children, young people and parents/carers using skills to elicit and impart relevant information. For example, responding to enquiries, taking and acting on referrals, talking to children in families they are working with. This includes accurate recording of information (knowing what to include and what to leave out.) This involves use of appropriate IT systems. Any recording should differentiate between fact and opinion.	*Communication* - use a range of routine skills and some advanced and specialised skills. *Communication* - use a range of IT applications to support and enhance work. *Practice* - Practise routine methods of enquiry.	Assessing needs and options in order to recommend a course of action: - Analyse the information they have gathered etc. Identifying and responding to crisis situations: - Understand the factors influencing the selection and testing of information.
	Students should have an understanding of the potential risks a child might be exposed to and how a child may attempt to convey his or her experiences using verbal or non verbal indicators. Practice teachers and tutors will be required to make clear links between the material on child development and communicating with children. Students need to be able to respond appropriately to the child and the information. This includes knowledge of child protection procedures and their roles and responsibilities, and the roles and responsibilities of other professionals.	*Knowledge* - knowledge that is detailed in some areas. *Practice* - Practise in a range of professional level contexts which include a degree of unpredictability. *Cognitive* - Draw on a range of sources in making judgements.	Work with individuals etc to achieve change, promote dignity, realise potential, improve life opportunities: - Communicate effectively across potential barriers resulting from differences in age, language, ability etc. Assessing and managing risks: - Understand social workers' roles as statutory agents. - Undertake practice in ways which tries to protect safety.
	Students should be able to demonstrate that they are clear about the purpose of contact with children and their responsibilities. For example, they should be able to articulate why they would see a child without his/her parents being present and what actions they could and would take (under guidance) if access was denied.	*Autonomy* - Work under guidance with qualified practitioners.	Assessing and managing risk: - Understand the concepts of rights, responsibility etc and the powers associated with the practice of social workers as moral and statutory agents.

	SCQF	Standards in Social Work Education
Level 9 – continued **Aim:** **Ability to demonstrate and use a selection of skills in contexts which include a degree of unpredictability.**	Where students are not in a practice learning opportunity where they have direct involvement with children or parents, there may need to be links with other agencies/ teams in order that the student can co-work/be allocated a case involving children or their parents. There are imaginative ways which practice teachers currently facilitate learning within and between teams and these methods can be built upon.	*Cognitive* - identify and analyse routine professional problems and issues. *Autonomy* - Practise in ways which take account of own and others' roles and responsibilities.	Assessing need and options: - Understand the models and methods of assessment in different practice contexts. Developing networks to meet assessed need and planned outcomes: - Develop effective helping relationships and partnerships.
	During practice learning opportunities, students need to have the opportunity to present information about child care and child protection both formally and informally. This might include making a presentation to a team meeting, a Children's Hearing, or a Case Conference.	*Communication* - make formal and informal presentations to a range of audiences.	Manage, present and share records and reports: - Present conclusions verbally and on paper in a structured form that is appropriate to the audience for which these have been prepared. Preparing for and taking part in decision making forums: - Make effective preparation for meetings and lead them in a productive way.

		SCQF	Standards in Social Work Education
Level 10 **Students will be expected to be competent in communicating at a professional level with peers and senior colleagues. This will include the ability to deliver formal presentations.**	By this stage, students should be competent in communicating with children, young people and their parents/carers and interpreting what children say (and do). This includes applying their knowledge about how children communicate to their practice. Where students do not undertake practice learning opportunities in child care settings, they need to be given specific opportunities to demonstrate their skills in communicating with children. In the report of the Inquiry into the death of Victoria Climbie, Lord Laming highlighted the fact that no social worker had ever got beyond asking Victoria "hello, how are you?" (2003, 65).	*Knowledge* - a critical understanding of the principal theories, concepts and principles.	Assessing needs and options: - Listen actively to people who use services and their carers respecting their experience and taking full account of their views.
	Formal meetings can understandably raise anxiety for children and their carers. Students need to be able to explain the purpose of such meetings in a manner which is aimed at decreasing anxiety. Children and families may need significant support within formal and informal settings to present their views, verbally or in written forms. Students should be able to facilitate children and parents to communicate their views.	*Practice* - use a range of principle skills, practices and/or materials associated with a subject or discipline.	Preparing for and take part in decision making forums: - Present evidence to decision making forums and help individuals, families etc to understand the procedures involved and the possible and actual outcomes. - Work with individuals, families, carers, groups and communities to select the best forms of representation and involvement in decision making. - Help individuals, families etc to be involved appropriately in decision making forums.
	Students will be required to demonstrate effective written communication: this would include production of written case recording/reports/assessments/letters to an appropriate standard and format. The importance of clear unambiguous written communication was also highlighted in the Laming Inquiry (2003) which stated that "staff must be held accountable for the quality of the information they provide" (1.43).	*Communication* - communicate with professional level peers, senior colleagues and specialists.	Managing, presenting and sharing records and reports: - Maintain accurate, complete, accessible and up to date records and reports. Preparing for and taking part in decision making forums: - Prepare reports and documents for decision making forums.

Level 10 – continued **Students will be expected to be competent in communicating at a professional level with peers and senior colleagues. This will include the ability to deliver formal presentations.**		SCQF	Standards in Social Work Education
	Students will be required to demonstrate that they have a clear understanding of their responsibility to effectively and accurately share information with other professionals, and children and their families in accordance with relevant guidance. For example Protecting Children - a Shared Responsibility (1998) or Getting Our Priorities Right (2003).	*Autonomy* - Practise in ways which shows a clear awareness of own and others roles and responsibilities.	Managing, presenting and sharing records: - Share records with individuals, families, carers etc within legal and ethical guidelines and requirements.
	It is recommended that students be required to make formal presentations in a variety of settings to a range of audiences. During practice learning opportunities students should demonstrate their ability to present their assessment, for instance, in a review, children's hearing, core group, or inter-agency meeting.	*Communication* - make formal presentations about specialised topics to informed audiences.	Preparing for and taking part in decision making forums: - Present evidence to decision making forums.
	Students should be able to articulate clearly and explicitly their skills and knowledge in relation to communication in a child care and child protection context to tutors, peers, practice teachers and future employers.	*Cognitive* - Critically review and consolidate knowledge, skills and practices and thinking.	Working within agreed standards of social work practice: - Critically reflect on their practice and performance and modify these as a result. Evaluating and using up to date knowledge of and research into social work practice: - Using supervision, consultancy and professional support take action to identify and meet their continuing professional development needs.

Knowledge and Understanding

During the course of their studies and practice learning opportunities, students will require to gain knowledge and demonstrate understanding in a number of key areas:

- The legal framework which underpins practice (both their own and other professionals)
- Relevant guidance
- Knowledge of theory and models of practice - including risk assessment
- Child care and protection in context
- Intra and inter agency practice

Level 7		SCQF	Standards in Social Work Education
Aim: **Students should demonstrate a broad knowledge of the key areas in child care and protection which will underpin practice.**	Students should be introduced to the legal frameworks which underpin practice. This will not be restricted to child care and protection as students will need a basic grounding in the legal context in which all social workers operate. However, they need to be made aware that there are some areas specific to child care and protection. For example they should be introduced to the Children (Scotland) Act 1995 and United Nations Convention on the Rights of the Child (1989).	*Knowledge* - A broad knowledge of the subject.	Preparing for social work contact and involvement: - Legal bases for intervention.
	Students need to be aware that in addition to legal frameworks, guidance exists at different levels. For example local child protection procedures, national guidance e.g. Protecting Children - a Shared Responsibility (1998). Students could be asked to explore how local child protection procedures might be applied to a case scenario.	*Knowledge* - A broad knowledge of the subject. *Practice* - Use some of the basic and routine professional skills, techniques, practices and/or materials associated with a subject.	Working within agreed standards of social work practice: - The significance of legislative and legal frameworks, service standards, practice guidelines and codes of practice.
	Students should be introduced to core theories which are relevant to social work practice generally. These will include theories which are particularly relevant to child care and protection. For example students could be encouraged to examine how sociological theory links to child care and protection and consider the impact of poverty on children.	*Knowledge* - Knowledge that is embedded in the main theories, concepts and principles. *Cognitive* - Use a range of approaches to address defined and/or routine problems and issues.	Working with individuals etc to achieve change, promote dignity, realise potential and improve life opportunities: - Psychological and physiological theories of individual and social development. Working with groups to promote choice: - The relevance of sociological and criminological perspectives to understanding societal and structural influences on human behaviour.

		SCQF	Standards in Social Work Education
Level 7 – continued **Aim:** **Students should demonstrate a broad knowledge of the key areas in child care and protection which will underpin practice.**	Students should be introduced to child care and protection in context. This will include an historical overview of key events and their impact on the development of social work practice. This would include the impact/development of specific areas of practice and exploring the changing culture within which social workers operate. This could include how the Maria Colwell Inquiry (1974) led to the development of child protection registers, the discourse surrounding the death of Jamie Bulger (1993), the impact of the Orkney Inquiry on current practice and legislation and the 21st Century Review: Changing Lives (2006). Students should be asked to reflect on how local practice may be affected by particular issues.	*Knowledge* - an awareness of the evolving/changing nature of knowledge and understanding. *Communication* - convey complex ideas in a well structured and coherent form.	Evaluating and using up-to-date knowledge and research into social work practice: - Factors influencing changes in practice within statutory, voluntary and private sector services.
	The SSSC Codes of Practice states that Social Workers should "recognise and respect the roles and expertise of workers from other agencies" (2003, 6.7). Students need to be aware of social work's place alongside other professionals. We recommend that this includes some taught input into different professionals' roles and responsibilities. Although this will be taught within a general context there will be specific core texts in relation to child care and protection which we recommend students read. This should include The Child Protection Audit and Review, "It's Everyone's Job to Make Sure I'm Alright" (2002).	*Autonomy* - Take account of own and others' roles and responsibilities in carrying out and evaluating tasks.	Developing networks to meet assessed needs and planned outcomes: - The significance of inter-relationships with other social services, especially education, housing, health etc.

	SCQF	Standards in Social Work Education
Level 8 **Aim:** **Students should demonstrate a broad knowledge of child care and protection with detailed knowledge in some areas. They should have some understanding of the core theories.**	Students should have knowledge and understanding of core legislation relating to child care and protection. For example, the legal definition of a child, parental rights and responsibilities, duties of the local authority, Children's Hearing System.	*Knowledge* - a broad knowledge of the scope, defining features and main areas of a subject	Tackling behaviour which presents a risk : - Students need to understand social workers' roles as statutory agents with duties and responsibilities to protect the public and uphold the law.
	Students would be taught more specifically about aspects of legislation relating to particular service user groups. For example they might explore how Anti-Social Behaviour Orders (2004) impact on children and young people and their families, and the role of the social worker.	*Knowledge* - Limited knowledge and understanding of some major current issues and specialisms.	Tackling behaviour which presents a risk: - Students need to understand the complex relationships between justice, care and control in social welfare and community justice and the practical and ethical effects of these.
	Students should build on their knowledge and understanding of relevant guidance. Regardless of where the student thinks they may practice or undertake their practice learning, they should have the opportunity within the HEI setting to apply relevant guidance to child care and protection case scenarios. For example, applying "Getting Our Priorities Right" (2003) to case scenarios where they take on the perspective of a criminal justice worker, mental health, children and families, etc.	*Practice* - Carry out routine lines of enquiry, development or investigation into professional level problems and issues. *Autonomy* - Take continuing account of own and others' roles, responsibilities and contributions in carrying out and evaluating tasks.	Assessing and managing risks: - Understanding the relationships between agency policies, legal and regulatory requirements and professional boundaries in shaping the nature of services provided in inter-disciplinary contexts.

		SCQF	Standards in Social Work Education
Level 8 – continued **Aim:** **Students should demonstrate a broad knowledge of child care and protection with detailed knowledge in some areas. They should have some understanding of the core theories.**	David Howe (1987) identified 3 reasons for being concerned with theory:- 1. Families prefer social workers - and other professionals - who are clear about what they are doing, why and how they are going to get there. 2. Different theories hold different assumptions about the nature of people and society and so inescapably lead to different types of practice. 3. Theories do not just appear - they are products of the society we live in - our ideas, beliefs and knowledge. Students should have knowledge of core theories relevant to child care and protection. Within the context of human growth and behaviour, students should gain specific knowledge and demonstrate understanding of normative child development, attachment theory, the impact of separation and loss.	*Generic* - Use a range of approaches to formulate evidence based solutions/responses. *Knowledge* - Understanding of a limited range of core theories, principles and concepts.	Assessing needs and options in order to recommend a course of action: - Assess human situations, taking account of a number of factors including the views of those involved, theoretical concepts, research evidence, legislation and organisational policies and procedures. Work with individuals etc to achieve change, promote dignity, realise potential and improve life opportunities: - Understand the nature, characteristics and effects of developmental delay, disruption and trauma and the significance of resilience.
	Students need to have some understanding of factors which will affect optimum development and increase vulnerability and risk - such as disability, diminished parenting capacity (because of substance misuse, mental health and domestic violence). Students need to develop an awareness of the range of substitute care and when it may be necessary to consider these options to protect children.	*Knowledge* - an outline knowledge and understanding of research. *Autonomy* - Manage resources within defined areas of work.	Evaluating and using up to date knowledge and research: - Assess the relative strength, applicability and implications of contrasting theories, explanations, research, policies, procedures and methods of intervention.

Level 8 – continued **Aim:** **Students should demonstrate a broad knowledge of child care and protection with detailed knowledge in some areas. They should have some understanding of the core theories.**	The Butler Sloss (1988) "Report of the enquiry into child abuse in Cleveland in 1987" stated: "…Childhood can be seen differently by the doctor, the teacher, the psychologist or the social worker. Because of all this is all too easy to view the child as an object of social intervention rather than as a person in their own right…" Students should explore different cultural concepts of childhood over time and place, including reflecting on their own experiences and how this might impact on practice. Horwath and Shardlow (2003) state "…there is continuing need to promote and encourage a wide and inclusive dialogue, across the profession as a whole." Students should start to demonstrate a clear understanding of their own and others roles, both within social work and across other agencies. For example they might 'role play' a case conference where they take on the role of another professional.	*Cognitive* - Undertake critical analysis, evaluation and/or synthesis of ideas, concepts, information and issues. *Communication* - convey complex information to a range of audiences and for a range of purposes. *Autonomy* - Take continuing account of own and others' responsibilities and contributions in carrying out and evaluating tasks.	Producing and implementing plans: - Understand the factors guiding the choice and evaluation of interventions in different circumstances. Producing and implementing plans: - Understand factors guiding the choice and evaluation of interventions in different circumstances.
		SCQF	**Standards in Social Work Education**

		SCQF	Standards in Social Work Education
Level 9 **Aim:** **Students should demonstrate a broad and integrated knowledge and understanding. They should demonstrate their ability to undertake critical analysis.**	Students need to be able to demonstrate that they can apply the legal framework to practice situations accurately and appropriately. Regardless of their practice learning setting, students will be expected to apply their knowledge of the responsibility of the local authority to children in need. For example, a worker in an adult mental health team would consider their responsibilities towards the child of a service user.	*Knowledge* - A broad and integrated knowledge and understanding of the scope, main areas and boundaries of a subject/discipline.	Working within agreed standards: - Understand the nature of legal authority, the application of legislation in practice.
	Students should be able to actively demonstrate how they have used relevant guidance in their practice learning opportunity.	*Cognitive* - Draw on a range of sources when making judgments.	Producing, implementing and evaluating plans: - Make decisions, set goals and develop specific plans taking account of relevant factors including professional guidance.
	Students should have the opportunity to learn and use models of assessment within the HEI setting. Within the general context of assessment we recommend that there is teaching on risk assessment in child care and protection. The Eilean Siar inspection report quoting from the Department of Health (2001) states "...any decision making requires a high level of professional judgment and qualitative assessment" (2005, 37). Consequently students should demonstrate their application of these models in practice learning settings. Key documents students ought to read would include DoH Framework for Assessment (2000) and the Scottish Executive Consultative Document, "Getting it Right for Every Child" (2005) which includes a comprehensive assessment framework.	*Knowledge* - Knowledge that is detailed in some areas and/or knowledge of one or more specialisms that are informed by forefront developments. *Practice* - Use a few skills, techniques , practices and/or materials that are specialised or advanced.	Tackling behaviour which presents a risk: - Understand models and methods of assessment, the use of relevant research, selecting and testing of relevant information, the nature of professional judgment and the processes of risk assessment and management.

	SCQF	Standards in Social Work Education
Level 9 – continued **Aim:** **Students should demonstrate a broad and integrated knowledge and understanding. They should demonstrate their ability to undertake critical analysis.**	Students should build on their knowledge of child development to identify key factors which increase vulnerability and risk and reduce resilience in children and young people. We recommend that students should receive specialist up to date teaching on the impact of substance misuse, domestic violence and mental health on parenting capacity and child development. Specialist practitioners might participate in the assessment of students as well as the delivery of material. The 21st Century Review (2006) recommended the development of "Practitioner Lecturers" and this may be helpful in ensuring that taught material continues to reflect practice issues. *Cognitive* - Undertake critical analysis, evaluation and/or synthesis of ideas, concepts, information and issues.	Assessing and managing risks: - Understand the nature of risks and harm associated with intervention in the lives of vulnerable, dangerous or socially excluded individuals and groups.
	Students need to demonstrate an understanding of the nature of long term intervention in child care and protection. For example, they should be familiar with Looked After Children (LAC) materials and guidance. Students need to have knowledge of the different forms of substitute care and make links to the teaching on child development, separation and loss. Students need to demonstrate that they have linked their knowledge about the potential for abuse in residential and foster care (perpetrated by adults or other children/ young people) to their role and responsibilities. *Knowledge* - A broad and integrated knowledge and understanding of the scope, main areas and boundaries of a subject/discipline.	Assessing and managing risks: - Analyse the nature of risks and potential for harm associated with the circumstances and nature of planned interventions.

	Standards in Social Work Education	SCQF	
Level 9 – continued **Aim:** **Students should demonstrate a broad and integrated knowledge and understanding. They should demonstrate their ability to undertake critical analysis.**	Students should develop their understanding of child care and protection in a changing context demonstrating how they have applied this to their practice. Students also need to demonstrate a critical understanding of how current social developments can influence policy and practice in relation to child care and protection. For example, students could research the impact of the Inquiry in to the death of Caleb Ness (O'Brien, 2004) on the child protection registration of infants.	*Practice* - Practise in a range of professional level contexts which include a degree of unpredictability.	Assessing and managing risks: - The complex relationships between public, social and political philosophies, policies and priorities and the organisation and practice of social work. Prepare for and take part in decision making forums: - Understand issues and trends in modern public and social policy and their relationship to contemporary practice and service delivery.
	Reder, Duncan and Gray highlighted that one feature which stood out of the 35 inquiries they reviewed was "flawed inter-agency communication" (1993, 60). In their practice learning opportunities and while at university students will be expected to demonstrate that they can translate effective inter-agency communication in to practice.	*Communication* - make formal and informal presentations on standard/ mainstream topics in the subject/ discipline to a range of audiences. *Autonomy* - Practise in ways which take account of own and others' roles and responsibilities.	Work effectively with professionals: - Analyse and work with the factors that inhibit integrated working across discipline, professional and agency boundaries. Work effectively with professionals: - Understand and take account of the views of others who are involved in collaborative work. Promoting best social work practice: - The effective management of potential conflicts created by codes and values held by different professional groups.

		SCQF	Standards in Social Work Education
Level 10 **Aim:** **Demonstrate detailed knowledge and critically apply this to practice.**	Students should now be able to demonstrate a thorough knowledge and understanding of legislation relevant to child care and protection and how the legislation applies to their practice. For instance, Children (Scotland) Act 1995, Fostering of Children (Scotland) Regulations 1996.	*Knowledge* - detailed knowledge and understanding in one or more specialisms.	Evaluating and using up to date knowledge: - Review and regularly update their own knowledge of relevant legislation, policy guidelines, service standards and procedural frameworks.
	By this stage in their academic career students should be able to show that they have accessed, read and understood core guidance and significant inquiry reports, and made links to their practice. One way students can evidence this is in their reflective learning logs.	*Knowledge* - knowledge and understanding of the ways in which the subject/discipline is developed.	Work within agreed standards of social work practice: - Work at all times within the professional codes of practice, ethical principles and service standards that underpin high quality social work practice.
	Students need to demonstrate a competent and critical understanding of principal theories in relation to child care and protection and clearly evidence how these underpin their practice. This means that they should approach their practice from a perspective which always takes cognisance of the needs of children.	*Knowledge* - a critical understanding of the principal theories, concepts and principles.	Evaluate and using up to date knowledge: - Locate, understand and critically evaluate research findings and literature that is relevant to social work practice.

Level 10 – continued **Aim:** **Demonstrate detailed knowledge and critically apply this to practice.**	SCQF	Standards in Social Work Education
The SSSC Codes of Practice (2003) state that social workers must follow "risk assessment policies and procedures to assess… take necessary steps to minimise the risks…. ensure relevant colleagues are informed" (4.2, 4.3, 4.4). We recommend that all students should be able to clearly demonstrate competence in assessment and intervention in child care and protection. This should include an ability to identify children in need or at risk and take appropriate action. Underpinning their assessment should be a sound knowledge base in relation to child development and parenting capacity.	*Practice* - use a few skills, practices and/or materials which are specialised, advanced, or at the forefront of a subject/discipline. *Practice* - Practise in a range of professional level contexts which include a degree of unpredictability and/or specialism.	Managing and presenting and sharing records: - Provide clear evidence for judgments and decisions. Assessing and managing risk: - Work within the risk assessment and management procedures of their own and other relevant organisations and professions. - Identify, assess and record the nature of risk, its seriousness and the harm it may cause. - Manage risk, regularly monitoring and re assessing priorities. Tackling behaviour which presents a risk: - Plan, manage and record intervention designed to change the identified risk behaviour. - Take prompt action to deal with behaviour or situations that present a risk.

25

		SCQF	Standards in Social Work Education
Level 10 – continued **Aim:** **Demonstrate detailed knowledge and critically apply this to practice.**	One of the comments from the Child Protection Audit "It's Everyone's Job to Make Sure I'm Alright" (Scottish Executive, 2002) was that there was limited evaluation of outcomes for children. Students need to demonstrate that their view of child care and protection places the child at the centre and focuses on his or her long term needs and that their intervention is predicated on evidence based practice.	*Cognitive* - Offer professional level insights, interpretations and solutions to problems and issues.	Managing one's own work in an accountable way: - Monitor and evaluate the appropriateness and effectiveness of their programmes of work in meeting the needs of individuals, families etc. Producing, implementing and evaluating plans: - Regularly review the effectiveness of plans with the people involved. Working with individuals etc to achieve change: - Understand research based concepts and critical explanations from social work theory and other disciplines that contribute to the knowledge base of social work including their reliability and how they are applied.
	Students will need to demonstrate during their practice learning opportunity that they can collaborate and undertake joint work with other professionals irrespective of their practice setting. This could include sharing their knowledge about child care and protection or drawing upon case knowledge and expertise of other professionals.	*Autonomy* - work with others to bring about change, development and/or new thinking. *Autonomy* - deal with complex ethical and professional issues in accordance with current professional and/or ethical codes of practice.	Preparing for social work contact and involvement: - Contact and work with relevant professionals and others to get additional information that can influence initial contact and involvement. Producing, implementing and evaluating plans: - Negotiate with others the services and resources that will be included in plans. Producing, implementing and evaluating plans: - Carry out their own responsibilities and monitor, coordinate and support the actions of others. Working effectively with professionals: - Work effectively with others in delivering integrated and multi disciplinary services.

Professionally Competent and Confident

In order to work effectively with children, young people, parents, carers, peers and other professionals, practitioners need to be competent and confident. This includes being clear about their professional role and responsibilities (and the limits of these). It also includes having a clear understanding about the professional responsibilities of others, and knowledge of when they need to draw on the services of others to improve outcomes for children, young people, parents and carers.

		SCQF	Standards in Social Work Education
Level 7 **Aim:** **Students should demonstrate an awareness of the concept of professional competence and confidence and exercise some initiative and independence.**	HEIs need to deliver teaching which explores the notion of a professional, and the role of a social worker. A key document which HEIs could use as a basis for group discussion is the '21st Century Review of Social Work', Changing Lives (2006).	*Knowledge* - a broad knowledge of the subject/discipline in general.	Promoting best social work practice: - The position of contemporary social work within historical and comparative perspectives. Working with individuals etc so they can make informed choices: - The nature of social work services in a diverse society.
	Students will have registered with the SSSC and need to start to demonstrate that they have some understanding of the implications of this with particular reference to child care and protection. For example, they should understand the need for Enhanced Disclosure and where the requirement fits within a range of policies to protect children.	There is no corresponding descriptor within the SCQF framework for this however it is a requirement.	Work within agreed standards of social work practice: - Work at all times within the professional codes of practice.
	Students need to be aware that personal responsibility is intrinsic to professional competence and confidence and they have a key responsibility for their own continuing professional development. Consequently they should be encouraged to identify gaps in knowledge and take responsibility for developing this knowledge base and keeping abreast of developments - by accessing research and literature. In line with the Framework for Social Work Education in Scotland (2003) we would recommend that students start professional development plans in their first year that they continue to build on through their academic career. Students may identify a lack of confidence in work with children, for example, and should explore how they might address this.	*Autonomy* - exercise some initiative and independence in carrying out defined activities at a professional level. *Autonomy* - take account of own and others' roles and responsibilities in carrying out and evaluating tasks.	Taking responsibility for one's own professional development: - Understand the importance of critical reflection and self monitoring in defining new personal learning plans.

	Standards in Social Work Education	SCQF	
Level 7 – continued **Aim:** **Students should demonstrate an awareness of concept of professional competence and confidence and exercise some initiative and independence.**	Students need to show an awareness of the meaning of professional boundaries and start to be able to make links between this and the appropriate use of authority. Within HEIs, students need to have an opportunity to use case scenarios to explore some of these issues. For example, when considering boundaries, students might be asked to consider how they would respond if a child sat on their knee during an initial home visit. Students need to start to consider their use of authority, employing case scenarios to start to practise this. We recommend that at least one of these scenarios should involve a child in need of protection.	*Practice* - use some of the basic and routine professional skills, techniques, practices… associated with a subject/discipline.	Managing one's own work in an accountable way: - Identify and keep under review personal and professional boundaries.
	Students need to be introduced to the concept of working in an organisation and could start to practise the skills this requires by undertaking exercises in a group. They need to be considering group dynamics and their responsibility within this. For example, in an organisation whose service users are adults, they would need to satisfy themselves that the organisation had appropriate recognition of the issues of child care and protection.	*Autonomy* - take account of own and others' roles and responsibilities in carrying out and evaluating tasks. *Autonomy* - work with others in support of current professional practice under guidance.	Evaluating and using up to date knowledge and research: - Employ understanding of human behaviour and intention at societal, organisational, community, inter-personal and intra-personal level.

		SCQF	Standards in Social Work Education
Level 8 **Aim:** **Students should demonstrate the ability to exercise autonomy and deal with professional issues under guidance.**	Students need to be given opportunities to develop confidence in their skills and take the initiative in defined areas of work. This could involve case scenarios where students are given particular responsibilities within the larger group. In this instance where students are learning with other professionals, for example in health or education, they could begin to explore power dynamics and professional integrity. A possible role play would be a child protection case conference, and links could be made to some of the findings of the O'Brien report in to the death of Caleb Ness (2003).	*Autonomy* - exercise autonomy and initiative in some activities at a professional level. *Autonomy* - take continuing account of own and others' roles and responsibilities and contributions in carrying out and evaluating tasks.	Working with groups: - Understand social science theories explaining group and organisational behaviour, adaptation and change. Working effectively with professionals: - Understand factors and processes facilitating effective service integration, interagency collaboration and partnership.
	Students need to have input into the value and purpose of supervision. In particular they need to be clear about the role of supervision on the decision making process. In relation to child care and protection, students should be equipped to expect a quality of supervision that will enable them to discuss complex and 'grey areas' of concern about a child's wellbeing. Students should expect that one of the purposes of supervision is to have their assessments challenged.	*Autonomy* - deal with ethical and professional issues in accordance with current professional and/or ethical codes of practice under guidance.	Managing one's own work in an accountable way: - Use professional and managerial supervision and support to improve their practice.
	Students need to have an understanding of the limits of the social work role and the responsibilities of other professionals. For example, adult service users may have misinformed views about the power social workers have to remove their children. This can inhibit honesty about the nature of a problem. Workers in all settings need to be aware of the range and limits of social work powers so that they can be accurate in their discussions with children, young people, parents, carers and other professionals.	*Knowledge* - a broad knowledge of the scope, defining features, and main areas of a subject/discipline.	Working within agreed standards: - Analyse and take account of the impact of inequality, discrimination and social exclusion in work with people in a wide range of contexts and problem situations.

		SCQF	Standards in Social Work Education
Level 8 – continued **Aim:** **Students should demonstrate the ability to exercise autonomy and deal with professional issues under guidance.**	Students need to become increasingly responsible for managing their own learning. For example, students might be asked to investigate what child protection procedures apply to a range of organisations, or whether different authorities have supervision policies. Every student going on practice learning opportunities should have read that agency's child protection procedures and be able to demonstrate that they are clear as to their responsibility (and its limits).	*Autonomy* - exercise autonomy and initiative in some activities at professional level. *Autonomy* - take the lead on planning in familiar or defined contexts.	Taking responsibility for one's own professional development: - Take responsibility for their own further and continuing acquisition of knowledge and skills.
	Students should have the opportunity to build on the initial input on the use of authority, with clear links made between this and the teaching on risk and vulnerability and intervention in childcare and protection.	*Knowledge* - detailed knowledge in some areas.	Tackling behaviour which presents a risk: - Plan for and manage situations in which there is a significant element of risk.
	Students should be able to start to demonstrate that they understand the concept of accountability and have started to think about how this would apply to their practice in relation to child care and protection. Case scenarios and role plays might be used to encourage students to clarify with tutors what they should do in particular instances - for example if they are involved in a home visit and a child is unattended.	*Autonomy* - work in support of current professional practice under guidance.	Identifying and responding to crisis situations: - Think logically even under pressure.

	SCQF	Standards in Social Work Education
Level 8 – continued **Aim:** **Students should demonstrate the ability to exercise autonomy and deal with professional issues under guidance.**	During practice learning opportunities, students will be required to make informal and formal presentations of their assessments, and they will be required to be given opportunities within HEIs to develop their confidence in this area. Students should be able to present information accurately and confidently in the HEI setting before going on a practice learning opportunity.	*Communication* - convey complex information to a range of audiences and for a range of purposes.	Preparing for and taking part in decision making forums: - Communicate clearly, accurately and precisely both verbally and in writing with individuals and groups in a range of formal and informal situations. Managing, presenting and sharing records and reports: - Write accurately and clearly in styles that are adapted to the audience, purpose and context of the communication.

Level 9 / Aim		SCQF	Standards in Social Work Education
Aim: **Students should be able to demonstrate broad and integrated levels of professional confidence and competence.**	By this stage students should be able to demonstrate both within a practice and academic setting that they are taking responsibility for their own professional development and practice. This means that they are prepared for supervision and tutorials and take some responsibility for contributing to the agenda. Specifically in relation to child care and protection they need to demonstrate that they see the relevance/centrality of this to their professional practice.	*Autonomy* - work under guidance with qualified practitioners. *Autonomy* - deal with ethical and professional issues in accordance with current professional and/or ethical codes of practices, seeking guidance where appropriate.	Taking responsibility for one's own professional development: - Reflect on and change their professional behaviour in the light of growing experience. Working within agreed standards: - Work in an open way and be able to justify their own actions within accepted ethical and professional standards.
	Students should be demonstrating that they can constructively challenge peers and other professionals. We recommend that HEIs and practice teachers make explicit links to child care and protection. A good example would be of 'Nurse 1' who did not agree that Caleb Ness should be discharged to his parents care and told the O'Brien Inquiry that she "did not appreciate that she should ask for her dissent to be recorded" (at the case conference), (O'Brien, 2003, 3.6.8).	*Cognitive* - undertake critical analysis, evaluation and/or synthesis of ideas, concepts, information and issues. *Autonomy* - exercise autonomy and initiative in some activities at a professional level.	Developing networks to meet assessed needs: - Challenge others when necessary in ways that are most likely to produce positive outcomes.
	Students should be able to explain the processes behind their assessment and intervention and demonstrate that they can critically evaluate the impact of their intervention and other's interventions. For example, if a decision is made that an adult requires to be detained under the Mental Health (Care and Treatment) Scotland Act 2003, they would need to demonstrate that the needs of any children had been fully considered.	*Knowledge* - a broad and integrated knowledge and understanding of the scope, main areas and boundaries of a subject/discipline.	Producing, implementing and evaluating plans: - Understand factors guiding the choice and evaluation of interventions in different circumstances. Identifying and responding to crisis situations: - Review outcomes taken in the light of actual outcomes. Evaluating and using up to date knowledge and research: - Monitor situations, review processes and evaluate outcomes.

33

		SCQF	Standards in Social Work Education
Level 10 **Aim:** **Students need to demonstrate they are confident and competent practitioners and can exercise initiative and autonomy**	A comment in the Child Protection Audit, 'It's Everyone's job to make sure I'm Alright' (2002) was that "some social workers had become inured" to the circumstances of particular children. Similarly, the Laming Report commented that, "the principal failure to protect her (Victoria) was the result of widespread organisational malaise" (2003, 1.21). One of the striking comments of a representative of a service user's group was that young people felt social workers made a difference when they were committed to the job. By this stage students need to demonstrate that they believe that they can make a difference to children, young people, their parents and carers and see themselves as "agents of change".	*Autonomy* - exercise autonomy and initiative in professional/ equivalent activities. *Autonomy* - work with others to bring about change, development and/or new thinking. *Cognitive* - offer professional level insights, interpretations and solutions. *Cognitive* - demonstrate some originality and creativity in dealing with professional level issues.	Working within agreed standards: - Exercise and justify their professional judgment.
	Students should be able to demonstrate to practice teachers and HEIs that they are clear about their professional role and responsibilities and are also clear as to the limits of their knowledge and responsibilities and when they need to share information with other professionals to protect a child.	*Autonomy* - practise in ways which show a clear awareness of own and others' roles and responsibilities. *Autonomy* - deal with complex ethical and professional issues in accordance with current professional and/or ethical codes of practice.	Identifying and responding to crisis: - Identify the need for statutory and procedural intervention. Promoting best social work practice: - Work with colleagues in related professions to develop and further integrate services. Contributing to the management of resources and services: - Contribute to procedures for managing and sharing information.

	SCQF	Standards in Social Work Education
Level 10 – continued **Aim:** **Students need to demonstrate they are confident and competent practitioners and can exercise initiative and autonomy.** Students should be confident in exercising their professional powers and responsibilities with reference to child care and protection. During their practice learning opportunity all students should have had the chance to present their assessment of a child/ young person or parent to an appropriate forum. (This may be formal or informal, some examples would be a Children's Hearing, Case conference, LAC review, team meeting, core group).	*Practice* - practise in a range of professional level contexts which include a degree of unpredictability and/or specialism. *Communication* - make formal presentations about specialised topics to informed audiences. *Communication* - communicate with professional level peers, senior colleagues and specialists.	Work within agreed standards: - Use appropriate assertiveness in justifying professional decisions and upholding social work practice values. Preparing for and taking part in decision making forums: - Present evidence to decision making forums.
Students need to demonstrate that they can exercise initiative and work autonomously. However they also need to demonstrate that they will seek appropriate support and guidance through supervision.	*Autonomy* - exercise autonomy and initiative in professional/ equivalent activities. *Autonomy* - work effectively under guidance in a peer relationship with qualified practitioners.	Managing one's own work in an accountable way: - Use professional and managerial supervision and support to improve their practice. Understanding and managing complex professional issues: - Act appropriately even in uncertain and ambiguous circumstances and critically reflect on and learn from the outcomes.

35

	SCQF	Standards in Social Work Education
Level 10 – continued **Aim:** **Students need to demonstrate they are confident and competent practitioners and can exercise initiative and autonomy.**	Students need to be competent and confident at translating their knowledge of risk assessment in to practice in child care and protection. This is reflected in the 21st Century Review Interim Report (2005) which states that social workers "need to be able to make complex decisions about the level of risk. This requires a high level of skill and personal autonomy and accountability"	*Knowledge* - detailed knowledge and understanding in one or more specialisms, some of which is informed by or a the forefront of a subject/discipline. *Practice* - practise in a range of professional level contexts which include a degree of unpredictability. *Cognitive* - critically identify, define, conceptualise and analyse complex/professional level problems and issues.	Tackling behaviour which presents a risk: - Work with individuals, families etc to : • Identify and evaluate situations and circumstances that may increase risks. • Reduce or contain the level of those risks.

Values and Ethical Practice

Although adopting social work values and practising in a manner which is ethical should underpin all practice with all service users, peers and other professionals, there are specific areas which are particularly relevant to child care and protection. All students will have been children, and will have experienced being parented, some students may well be parents themselves. Students own experiences (of childhood and being parented or parenting) will have contributed to who they are and their values. In some instances this will be helpful to them as practitioners, in other instances it may not. In all instances students need to reflect on their own values and take responsibility to make change where these are in conflict with core social work values.

		SCQF	Standards in Social Work Education
Level 7 **Aim:** **Students should demonstrate an awareness of social work values and ethical practice.**	Students will be expected to demonstrate a readiness to reflect on their own values and experiences and consider the impact these may have on their assessment and intervention generally. Specific to child care and protection they will be expected to start to consider the relevance of their own attachment experiences/experience of parenting to their future practice. For example, students should be asked to reflect on their own experience and views of discipline and how these may influence their practice in the context of current legal frameworks.	*Knowledge* - An understanding of the difference between explanations based on evidence and/or research and other forms of explanation and the importance of this difference.	Representing in partnership with others to help them achieve and maintain greater independence: - Overcome personal prejudices to respond appropriately to a range of complex personal and interpersonal situations.
	As a foundation for ethical practice students require taught input on social work values. The 21st Century Review Report 'Changing Lives' states that "Social work is based on respect for the inherent worth and dignity of all people and the rights that flow from this...." (2006). Students should be expected to read this and other key documents and to consider how they apply to children, young people, parents and carers.	*Knowledge* - knowledge that is embedded in the main theories, concepts and principles. *Practice* - Use some of the basic and routine professional skills, techniques, practices and/or materials associated with the subject/discipline.	Working within agreed standards: - Understand the nature, historical development and application of social work values and codes of practice.
	Students should be introduced to the concept of anti-discriminatory/anti-oppressive practice and this should include child care and protection case scenarios.	*Knowledge* - knowledge that is embedded in the main theories, concepts and principles.	Working within agreed standards: - Analyse and take account of the impact of inequality, discrimination and social exclusion. Assessing and managing risks: - Up to date legislation defining the rights of people, especially measures designed to tackle all forms of discrimination.

Level 7 – continued **Aim:** **Students should demonstrate an awareness of social work values and ethical practice.**	Most HEIs have developed links with service users and carers and they should have some input to the student's early learning opportunities. We recommend that one of the areas explored highlights how service users have experienced social work intervention. As it may be difficult for children and parents currently involved in the child protection system to speak about their experiences, HEIs may need to employ other resources (video, DVD, audio tape) to ensure that this group is represented.	*Knowledge* - Knowledge that is embedded in the main theories, concepts and principles. *Cognitive* - Use a range of approaches to address defined and/or routine problems and issues within familiar contexts.	Preparing for and taking part in decision making forums: - Understand factors that inhibit effective participation in decision making in different settings. Working with groups to promote choice: - Involve users of social work services etc.
		SCQF	**Standards in Social Work Education**

		SCQF	Standards in Social Work Education
Level 8 **Aim:** **Students need to demonstrate a broad awareness of values and ethics and deal with ethical issues in accordance with professional/ethical codes (SSSC Codes of Practice, 2003).**	All students should be encouraged to reflect on the importance of ethical practice in child care and protection. Using case examples from different practice settings they will need to demonstrate that while balancing the needs of children and their parents, they can ensure the child's needs remain paramount.	*Autonomy* - deal with ethical and professional issues in accordance with current professional and/or ethical codes or practices under guidance.	Identifying and responding to crisis situations: - Understanding factors influencing the selection and testing of relevant information.
	Students will be expected to show that they can demonstrate social work values in their learning relationships with their peers and teaching staff as well as service users and carers. Students who cannot treat their fellow students with dignity and respect should not have access to service users and carers and may not be able to progress with their studies.	*Autonomy* - work in support of current professional practice under guidance.	Manage one's own work in an accountable way: - Handle inter-personal and intra-personal conflict constructively.
	In group and individual tutorials students will be expected to reflect in more depth on their experiences and the "use of self" in their practice. Students might also consider this in reflective logs. Students should expect to be challenged if they express views which are in conflict with social work values. The focus of this is that as practitioners they will need to be able to provide a professional service to a range of service users whose circumstances, behaviour or views may challenge their value base. This might include adults, children and young people who exhibit sexually harmful behaviour, asylum seekers and their children, substance misusing parents.	*Knowledge* - a broad knowledge of the scope, defining features, and main areas of a subject/discipline. *Cognitive* - Undertake critical analysis, evaluation and/or synthesis of ideas, concepts, information and issues which are within the common understandings of the subject/discipline. *Autonomy* - Work in support of current professional practice under guidance.	Promoting best social work practice: - Reflect critically on their own conduct and practice, identifying the need for change. Take responsibility for one's own professional development: - Make a positive contribution to the continuing education of colleagues. Promoting best social work practice: - Challenge unacceptable practices in a responsible manner.

Level 8 – continued **Aim:** **Students need to demonstrate a broad awareness of values and ethics and deal with ethical issues in accordance with professional/ethical codes (SSSC Codes of Practice, 2003).**	Prior to the assessed practice learning opportunity students will be required to demonstrate that they are clear about the nature of professional boundaries and this could be explored using role play. For example, what would they do if an adult they were working with disclosed to them they had been sexually abused by a family member and they were worried about their 6 year old niece having contact with this person, but asked them "not to say anything"?	*Autonomy* - Deal with ethical and professional issues in accordance with current professional and/or ethical codes or practices under guidance. *Practice* - Carry out routine lines of enquiry, development or investigation into professional level problems and issues.	Work effectively with professionals: - Function effectively within a framework of complex accountability. Understanding and managing complex ethical dilemmas: - Analyse and handle ethical dilemmas and conflicts to produce clear accountable outcomes.
		SCQF	**Standards in Social Work Education**

		SCQF	Standards in Social Work Education
Level 9 **Aim:** **Students have a critical understanding of a range of skills enabling them to demonstrate ethical practice.**	During their practice learning opportunity and whilst at HEI, students must demonstrate that they can practise ethically. This means that they have been observed treating service users and carers with respect, promoting dignity.	*Practice* - Use a selection of the principle skills, techniques, practices and/or materials associated with a subject/discipline. *Autonomy* - Practise in ways which take account of own and others' roles and responsibilities.	Work within agreed standards: - Work in an open way and be able to justify their own actions within accepted ethical and professional standards.
	Students need to demonstrate that they are aware of the impact of discrimination on service users and have taken responsibility to challenge this in an appropriate way. With reference to child care and protection, students need to demonstrate that they are aware of how children can be particularly discriminated against and how this can add to their vulnerability. For example, Kennedy states "large numbers of disabled children use an alternative form of communication and a range of methods to communicate" (in Wilson and James 2004, 152) and in her research found practitioners did not have the skills to communicate. Students need to show they are aware of their responsibility to access additional support services.	*Knowledge* - A critical understanding of a selection of the principle theories, principles, concepts and terminology. *Practice* - Use a few skills, techniques, practices and/or materials that are specialised or advanced. *Autonomy* - Deal with ethical and professional issues in accordance with current professional and/or ethical codes or practices, seeking guidance where appropriate.	Working with individuals etc so that they can make informed decisions: - Consider specific factors that are relevant to social work practice, such as risk, resilience, rights, cultural, racial and ethnic identity etc and responsibilities to protect vulnerable individuals. Understanding and managing complex ethical issues: - Challenge individual, institutional and structural discrimination in constructive ways.

Level 9 – continued **Aim:** **Students have a critical understanding of a range of skills enabling them to demonstrate ethical practice.**		SCQF	Standards in Social Work Education
	Building on previous input on balancing the needs of children and their parents, students should demonstrate, either in practice or using case studies, that they can continue to work in an environment where the views of the service user may be in conflict with their assessment and subsequent actions. For example, a student working in a drug and alcohol team may disagree with the parent's own assessment of the impact of their substance misuse on parenting capacity.	*Knowledge* - knowledge that is detailed in some areas and/or knowledge of one or more specialisms that are informed by forefront developments. *Autonomy* - Exercise autonomy and initiative in some activities at a professional level. *Autonomy* - Deal with ethical and professional issues in accordance with current professional and/or ethical codes or practices, seeking guidance where appropriate.	Tackling behaviour which presents a risk: - The complex relationships between justice, care and control and social welfare and community justice and the practical and ethical effects of these.
	Students need to demonstrate while on practice learning opportunities that they have achieved a balance between treating service users with respect and dignity and not being over familiar. The SSSC Codes of Practice reflects this noting that social workers must not "form inappropriate personal relationships with service users" (2003, 5.4). Students need to be clear about the personal/professional boundaries. An example would be that it would be inappropriate for them to offer to provide substitute care for a vulnerable child in response to a lack of resources.	*Knowledge* - A broad and integrated knowledge and understanding of the scope, main areas and boundaries of a subject/discipline. *Cognitive* - Identify and analyse routine professional problems and issues. *Autonomy* - Deal with ethical and professional issues in accordance with current professional and/or ethical codes or practices, seeking guidance where appropriate.	Managing one's own work in an accountable way: - Identify and keep under review personal and professional boundaries. Promoting best social work practice: - Reflect critically on own conduct and practice, identifying the need for change.

Level 10 **Students demonstrate ethical practice based on SSSC Codes of Practice (2003).**		SCQF	Standards in Social Work Education
	By this stage, students should be able to assess and intervene appropriately in complex situations where they identify that a child may be in need or at risk. This means that they can prioritise the needs of a child irrespective of who their primary client is.	*Knowledge* - detailed knowledge and understanding in one or more specialisms, some of which is informed by or at the forefront of a subject/discipline. *Practice* - practise in a range of professional level contexts which include a degree of unpredictability and/or specialism. *Cognitive* - offer professional level insights, interpretations and solutions to problems and issues.	Understanding and managing complex ethical issues: - Identify, understand and critically evaluate ethical issues, dilemmas and conflicts affecting their practice. Tackling behaviour which presents a risk: - Take prompt action to deal with behaviour or situations that present a risk. Tackling behaviour which presents a risk: - Plan, manage and record intervention designed to change the identified risk behaviour positively.
	Students need to demonstrate that they are aware of their own personal values in relation to child care and protection and if necessary can separate these from their practice to ensure they respond professionally. Students need to demonstrate that where there is a conflict between their personal and professional values, they can use supervision effectively to address this.	*Knowledge* - A critical understanding of the principal theories, concepts and principles. *Autonomy* - Deal with complex ethical and professional issues in accordance with current professional and/or ethical codes of practice. *Autonomy* - work effectively under guidance in a peer relationship with qualified practitioners.	Understanding and managing complex ethical issues: - Devise effective strategies to deal with ethical issues, dilemmas and conflicts. Managing one's own work in an accountable way: - Use professional and managerial supervision and support to improve their practice.

Level 10 – continued		SCQF	Standards in Social Work Education
Students demonstrate ethical practice based on SSSC Codes of Practice (2003).	Students need to be aware that their professional assessment of a child's needs may be in conflict with that of the agency providing their practice learning opportunity. They need to demonstrate an ability to challenge appropriately to ensure that they discharge their professional responsibility. For example, where students believe the agency's overall assessment is based on resource rather than need, they have a professional responsibility to confront this using appropriate channels.	*Cognitive* - Offer professional level insights, interpretations and solutions to problems and issues. *Communication* -communicate with professional level peers, senior colleagues and specialists. *Autonomy* - Exercise autonomy and initiative in professional/equivalent activities.	Working effectively with professionals: - Deal constructively with disagreements and conflict within work relationships. Promoting best social work practice: - Use supervision together with other organisational and professional systems to influence courses of action where practice falls below the standards required.
	While discharging their authority, students may encounter aggression or abuse from service users. For example, parents may be angry where the student has acted on a concern for a vulnerable child. Students need to demonstrate that they can seek appropriate supervision to ensure that their professional assessment and intervention is not compromised. Students need to be clear that it is not acceptable to carry out their duties in an unsafe environment and they need to be clear of the agency's responsibility to put in place reasonable safeguards to protect them. Notwithstanding this, the needs of any children should be paramount. For example, if a student decides it is not safe to visit a child at home because s/he hears a violent argument as s/he approaches, the student should seek immediate guidance about the needs of children in the house. This might involve a referral to other professionals (e.g. police).	*Practice* - practise in a range of professional level contexts which include a degree of unpredictability and/or specialism. *Cognitive* - Critically review and consolidate knowledge, skills and practices and thinking in a subject/discipline. *Cognitive* - Make judgements where information is limited or comes from a range of sources. *Autonomy* - work effectively under guidance in a peer relationship with qualified practitioners.	Assessing and managing risks: - Assess, analyse and record potential risk to themselves and colleagues. Assessing and managing risks: - Practise in ways that maximise safety and effectiveness especially in situations of uncertainty or if there is incomplete information. Understanding and managing complex ethical issues: - Act appropriately even in uncertain and ambiguous circumstances and critically reflect on and learn from the outcomes. Assessing and managing risks: - Manage risk to individuals, etc, regularly monitoring and re-assessing priorities.

	SCQF	Standards in Social Work Education
Level 10 – continued **Students demonstrate ethical practice based on SSSC Codes of Practice (2003).**	MacDonald and Winkley state: "Every child has the right to expect that professionals intervening in their lives will do so on the basis of the best available knowledge" (2000, 1). Students need to be clear that in order to practice in an ethical manner their methods should be based on the best evidence of what works for children and that they are responsive to new ideas from research.	*Knowledge* - detailed knowledge and understanding in one or more specialisms, some of which is informed by or at the forefront of a subject/discipline. *Practice* - Use a range of the principal skills, practices and/or materials associated with a subject/discipline. *Autonomy* - work with others to bring about change, development and/or new thinking.	Managing one's own work in an accountable way: - Carry out duties accountably, using professional judgement and knowledge based social work practice. Evaluating and using up to date knowledge and research: - Use professional and organisational supervision and support to research, critically analyse and review the evidence base for effective practice.
	Students should be aware of the outcomes of their intervention including unintended outcomes. For example, while it may support parents with learning difficulties to provide extensive home care from a range of professionals, this may have the unintended outcome of increasing their child's vulnerability and attachment difficulties.	*Knowledge* - A critical understanding of the principal theories, concepts and principles. *Practice* - practise in a range of professional level contexts which include a degree of unpredictability and/or specialism. *Autonomy* - Deal with complex ethical and professional issues in accordance with current professional and/or ethical codes of practice.	Assessing and managing risks: - Review intentions and actions in the light of expected and unintended consequences. Assessing and managing risks: - Plan, monitor, review and record outcomes and actions taken to minimise risk, stress and harm.

POST-GRADUATE ROUTE

SCQF levels

A number of post-graduate routes to professional social work qualification are available in Scotland. These vary in terms of the SCQF levels at which they are taught and assessed. Within Key Capabilities the post-graduate route has been aligned to level 10 in terms of academic work and practice competence.

The post-graduate routes are shorter and therefore as students are studying and practising over a 2-year, rather than a 4-year, period the incremental nature of the Key Capabilities will need to be adjusted.

Key Capabilities have not been separated into years one and two. Rather, the different areas in relation to child care and protection which students need to cover in the course of their academic study and practice learning have been identified.

Key Capabilities

1) Effective Communication
2) Knowledge and Understanding
3) Professional Confidence and Competence
4) Values and Ethical Practice

	POST-GRADUATE ROUTE	SCQF Level 10	Standards in Social Work Education
Effective Communication	Effective communication underpins all social work intervention. Because of their previous studies, students should already be able to demonstrate that they can communicate effectively with peers and make formal presentations; however they will require specific teaching on the differences in communicating with children and adults. While some skills are transferable, some areas of communication will be new to students. For example, it is unlikely that a science/engineering graduate will have studied how children communicate and some students will require significant input. All students will need to show knowledge of and demonstrate good listening and communication skills (including verbal and non-verbal communication). As the SSSC Codes of Practice notes social workers should communicate in an "appropriate, open, accurate and straightforward way" (2003, 2.2).	*Knowledge and Understanding* - a critical understanding of the principal theories, concepts and principles.	Assessing needs and options: - Listen actively to people who use services and their carers, respecting their experience and taking full account of their views.
	Prior to their first practice learning opportunity, students will be required to demonstrate that they understand the purpose of communicating with children, young people, their parents and carers. They will also need to demonstrate that they have the required skills in order to do this effectively on their practice learning opportunity. One way that this may be assessed is by recording videos of students in role play which are assessed by tutors and service user representatives. During their practice learning opportunity, students will be assessed on their ability to engage and relate effectively and form and maintain working relationships based on honesty and partnership.	*Practice* - use a range of the principal skills, practices associated with a subject/discipline.	Preparing for social work contact and involvement: - Engage and relate effectively with people who use services, with their families and other carers and with other professionals, maintaining awareness of their own style and approach and its effect on others.

	POST-GRADUATE ROUTE	SCQF Level 10	Standards in Social Work Education
Effective Communication	Students need to demonstrate that they have a clear understanding that children may convey their experiences using verbal and non-verbal indicators. Through their behaviour or their presentation a child may be communicating their needs and conveying their experiences. Therefore in order to assess accurately students need to have a good knowledge of child development and an awareness of the importance of observing children. Students need to demonstrate that they can use both verbal and non-verbal cues to guide interpretation of behaviour and help assess risk. One way to describe this is "listening with your eyes". Tutors and practice teachers should make explicit links between the material on child development and the skills required to communicate with children.	*Knowledge and understanding* - detailed knowledge and understanding in one or more specialisms.	Preparing for social work involvement: - Evaluate all information to identify the best form of initial involvement. Evaluating and using up to date knowledge and research into social work practice: - Implement knowledge based social work approaches and methods to develop and improve their own practice.
	Students will be required to demonstrate that they can use a range of communication skills to both elicit and analyse relevant information.	*Cognitive* - Offer professional level insights interpretations and solutions to problems and issues.	Working with individuals etc so they can make informed decisions: - Work with individuals etc to identify, gather and analyse relevant information.
	Students need to show that they can transfer their written skills to child care and protection work, and need to demonstrate that they can accurately record relevant information in a manner which is easily understood. For example, HEIs might adopt a baseline that if written material is not of a standard which would be acceptable to a Children's Hearing or a Sheriff Court then it is not acceptable to the university.	*Practice* - Use a range of principal, practices and/or materials associated with a subject or discipline. *Communication* - use a wide range of routine skills.	Managing, presenting and sharing records and reports: - Maintain accurate, complete, accessible and up to date records and reports. Preparing for and taking part in decision making forums: - Prepare reports and documents for decision making forums such as courts, hearings, case conferences.

	POST-GRADUATE ROUTE	SCQF Level 10	Standards in Social Work Education
Effective Communication	The need for clear unambiguous communication, and their responsibility to communicate effectively (including the appropriate sharing of information with children, young people, parents, carers, peers and other professionals) should be explicit in the teaching and assessment. We recommend that practice teachers and tutors make clear links to the limitations in communication mentioned by Inquiry Reports. We recommend that relevant reports and Guidance (For example, Protecting Children - A Shared Responsibility, 1998) should be required reading for students. Students could demonstrate that they have critically appraised the messages from inquiry reports in their learning log.	*Practice* - use a few skills and/or materials which are specialised. *Communication* - Communicate with professional level peers, senior colleagues and specialists. *Autonomy* - Practise in ways which show a clear awareness of own and others role and responsibilities.	Work within agreed standards of social work practice: - Work at all times within the professional codes of practice, ethical principles and service standards that underpin high quality social work practice. Managing, presenting and sharing records and reports: - Share records with individuals/families etc within legal and ethical guidelines and requirements.
	Students need to be able to demonstrate that they can communicate effectively to a range of audiences using appropriate methods. Students might role play how they would explain their assessment, that for his/her needs to be met, a child needs alternative long-term care, to: • A 6 year old child • A parent who has been defined as having learning difficulties • A Child Protection Case Conference	*Practice* - Practise in a range of professional level contexts which include a degree of unpredictability and/or specialism. *Communication* - communicate with professional level peers, senior colleagues and specialists.	Working with individuals etc so they can make informed decisions: - Work with individuals, families etc to: • inform them of their right and responsibilities • clarify and explain the social work organisation's duties, services and responsibilities.
	At the point of qualifying students need to show that they can communicate effectively in group situations (for example Case Conference) within their own agency and across other relevant disciplines.	*Communication* - make formal presentations about specialised topics to informed audiences.	Preparing for and taking part in decision making forums: - Present evidence to decision making forums and help individuals, families etc to understand the procedures involved and the possible and actual outcomes.

	POST-GRADUATE ROUTE	SCQF Level 10	Standards in Social Work Education
Effective Communication	Students will be required to demonstrate that they have appropriate knowledge and skills in communicating with children and their parents/carers where English is not the first language or where the primary form of communication is non-verbal. Students need to demonstrate knowledge of their responsibilities and competence in transferring this responsibility to their practice.	*Autonomy* - Deal with complex ethical and professional issues in accordance with current professional and/or ethical codes of practice.	Preparing for and taking part in decision making forums: - Help individuals/families to be involved appropriately in decision making forums. Working with individuals etc to achieve change, promote dignity, realise potential and improve life opportunities: - Develop relationships with individuals, families etc that show respect for diversity, equality etc. Work within agreed standards of social work practice: - Work at all times within the professional codes of practice, ethical principles and service standards that underpin high quality social work practice.
	For students who are not in a practice learning opportunity where they have direct contact with children, we recommend that they have the opportunity to be allocated or co-work a case involving a child or a parent. Some HEIs have child observation, and while this is a good foundation, at the point of qualifying students should have done more than observe a child. They should have had the opportunity to undertake an assessment of a child's circumstances and "offer professional level insights, interpretations and solutions" (Level 10, SCQF, 2003).	*Generic* - Offer professional level insights interpretations and solutions to problems and issues.	Assessing needs and options: - Identify, evaluate and recommend appropriate courses of action for individuals, families, carers etc.

Knowledge and Understanding	POST-GRADUATE ROUTE	SCQF Level 10	Standards in Social Work Education
	Because of their previous academic study students have demonstrated that they have knowledge and understanding in a particular area. This may or may not be related to the knowledge and understanding they will require to be effective qualified social workers. During the course of their studies and practice leaning opportunities, students will require to gain knowledge and understanding in the following key areas: • The legal framework which underpins practice • Relevant guidance and policy • Knowledge of theory and models of practice - including risk assessment • Child care and protection in context • Intra and inter agency practice The legal frameworks and guidance which underpin practice should form a key area of teaching and assessment. In addition students will need to have a good understanding of the policies and guidance which also define their responsibilities in relation to child care and protection. Students should be assessed on their knowledge of these prior to undertaking their first practice learning opportunity. This should ensure that all students undertaking practice learning will have a basic knowledge and understanding of their legal responsibilities and basis for intervention.	*Knowledge* - knowledge that covers and integrates most of the principal areas, features, boundaries etc of the subject. *Knowledge* - detailed knowledge and understanding in one or more specialisms.	Identifying and responding to crisis : - Identify the need for statutory and procedural intervention. Evaluating and using up to date knowledge and research into social work practice: - Review and regularly update their own knowledge of relevant legislation, policy guidelines etc.

	POST-GRADUATE ROUTE	SCQF Level 10	Standards in Social Work Education
Knowledge and Understanding	Some of the key documents students should know about, and know how to access will include the Children (Scotland) Act 1995, United Nations Convention on the Rights of the Child 1989, Getting Our Priorities Right, 2003. Students should have access to examples of local authority Child Protection Committee Child Protection Procedures and Children's Services Plans. At the point of qualifying, students should be able to demonstrate that they have accessed, read and understood core legislation, guidance and inquiry reports and can make links to their own practice. Students can evidence their critical understanding of the above in their reflective learning logs.	*Knowledge* - Knowledge and understanding of the ways in which the subject/discipline is developed. *Autonomy* - practise in ways which show a clear awareness of own and others roles and responsibilities.	Evaluating and using up to date knowledge and research: - Locate, understand and critically evaluate findings and literature that is relevant to social work practice.
	During their practice learning opportunities students need to be able to demonstrate that they can apply the legal framework to practice situations accurately and appropriately. Regardless of the practice learning opportunity setting, students will be required to apply their knowledge of the responsibility of all social workers towards children in need. For example, a worker in an adult mental health team would consider their responsibilities towards the child of a service user. Students should be able to actively demonstrate how they have used relevant guidance in their practice learning settings.	*Practice* - use a few skills, practices and/or materials which are specialised.	Assessing needs and options: - Assess and evaluate needs, strengths, risks and options, taking account of legal and other duties and service standards requirements. Work within agreed standards of social work practice: - Exercise and justify their professional judgment.

	POST-GRADUATE ROUTE	SCQF Level 10	Standards in Social Work Education
Knowledge and Understanding	Having previously studied to degree level, students will have already demonstrated that they have a "critical understanding of theories, concepts and principles." (Level 10 SCQF, 2003). However, dependant on their previous area of study these will not necessarily be applicable to social work. David Howe (1987) identified 3 reasons for being concerned with theory:- 1. Families prefer social workers - and other professionals - who are clear about what they are doing, why and how they are going to get there 2. Different theories hold different assumptions about the nature of people and society and so inescapably lead to different types of practice. 3. Theories do not just appear - they are products of the society we live in – our ideas, beliefs and knowledge.	*Knowledge* - Critical understanding of the principal theories, concepts and principles.	Evaluating and using up to date knowledge and research: - Locate, understand and critically evaluate research findings and literature that is relevant to social work practice.
	Students require to have input on theories of individual and social development. Within the context of human growth and behaviour students should have knowledge of core theories relevant to child care and protection. These include but are not restricted to attachment theory, separation and loss, resilience and adversity. Students should also have an understanding of how sociological perspectives have relevance for child care and protection. For example students need to explore the impact of poverty on children and their parents/carers.	*Knowledge* - Critical understanding of the principal theories, concepts and principles.	Evaluating and using up to date knowledge and research: - Implement knowledge based social work approaches and methods to develop and improve their own practice.
	Regardless of where they undertake their practice learning opportunities, students need to demonstrate a competent and critical understanding of principle theories in relation to child care and protection and clearly evidence how these underpin their practice. This means that they should approach their practice from the perspective which always takes cognisance of the needs of the child.	*Knowledge* - Critical understanding of the principal theories, concepts and principles.	Working within agreed standards of social work practice: - Exercise and justify their professional judgment.

Knowledge and Understanding	POST-GRADUATE ROUTE	SCQF Level 10	Standards in Social Work Education
	Students should build on their knowledge of child development to identify key factors which increase vulnerability and risk and reduce resilience in children and young people. We recommend that students receive specialist up to date teaching on the impact of substance misuse, domestic violence and mental health on parenting capacity and child development. In terms of assessing learning, one possibility would be to involve specialist practitioners in the assessment process.	*Cognitive* - Critically identify, define, conceptualise and analyse complex problems and issues. *Cognitive* - offer professional level insights, interpretations and solutions to problems and issues.	Evaluating and using up to date knowledge and research: - Implement knowledge based social work approaches and methods to develop and improve their own practice. Work effectively with professionals: - Work effectively with others in delivering integrated and multi-disciplinary services.
	Students need to demonstrate an understanding of the nature of long term intervention in child care and protection. We recommend students should be familiar with Looked After Children materials and guidance. Students need to have knowledge of the different forms of substitute care and be able to make links to the teaching on child development, separation and loss.	*Autonomy* - Work with others to bring about change, development and / or new thinking. *Practice* - Practise in a range of professional level contexts which include a degree of unpredictability and/or specialism.	Managing one's own work in an accountable way: - Monitor and evaluate the appropriateness and effectiveness of their programme of work in meeting the needs of individuals etc. Producing, implementing and evaluating plans: - Regularly review the effectiveness of plans with the people involved.

	POST-GRADUATE ROUTE	SCQF Level 10	Standards in Social Work Education
Professional Confidence and Competence	The inspection into the care and protection of children in Eilean Siar, states "High quality confident staff are necessary to protect children and help their families" (SWIA 2005, 78). Early in their training, students should be exploring the notion that personal responsibility and accountability is intrinsic to professional competence and confidence. Students need to demonstrate that they are able to take responsibility for their own continuing professional development. The expectation is that students will actively identify gaps in their knowledge base or areas where they lack confidence and with the support of academic staff and practice teachers, take steps to address these. For example students may identify a lack of confidence in how to respond appropriately to a child protection referral. In this instance students would be expected to identify relevant procedures and guidance and apply them to a case scenario.	*Autonomy* - Exercise autonomy and initiative in professional activities. *Autonomy* - work effectively under guidance in a peer relationship with qualified practitioners.	Managing one's own work in an accountable way: - Carry out duties accountably, using professional judgment and knowledge based social work practice. Managing one's own work in an accountable way: - Use professional and managerial supervision and support to improve their practice.
	Students must be able to demonstrate to practice teachers and HEIs that they are clear about their professional role and responsibilities and are also clear as to the limits of their knowledge and responsibilities and when they need to share information with other professionals to protect a child or include information from other sources in their assessment. In addition, they need to recognise that the act of sharing information does not in itself constitute action to protect. Here the lessons from Eilean Siar need to be learned "Gathering together large amounts of information is not an assessment. Sharing it does not constitute a child protection plan" (SWIA 2005, 77).	*Autonomy* - Practise in ways which show a clear awareness of own and others' roles and responsibilities.	Producing, implementing and evaluating plans: - Carry out their own responsibilities and monitor, co-ordinate and support the actions of others involved in putting plans in to practice. Promoting best social work practice: - Work with colleagues in related professions to develop and further integrate services. Working within agreed standards: - Exercise and justify their professional judgment.

	POST-GRADUATE ROUTE	SCQF Level 10	Standards in Social Work Education
Professional Confidence and Competence	Students have a responsibility to register with the professional body and need to demonstrate that they have an understanding of the implications of this in relation to child care and protection.	There is no corresponding descriptor within the SCQF framework for this however it is a requirement for practice.	Working within agreed standards of social work practice: - Work at all times within the professional codes of practice, ethical principles and service standards that underpin high quality social work practice.
	Students should be expected to reflect critically on their own practice and conduct and on the practice and conduct of others, maintaining a focus on the needs of service users. Irrespective of whether the student's primary responsibility is to an adult service user or his/her child, the student needs to demonstrate that they can objectively consider the needs of both and identify and intervene where these needs may conflict.	*Autonomy* - recognise the limits of codes and seek guidance where appropriate.	Working within agreed standards of social work practice: - Critically reflect on their practice and performance and modify these as a result.

	POST-GRADUATE ROUTE	SCQF Level 10	Standards in Social Work Education
Professional Confidence and Competence	Students need to demonstrate that they are clear about the importance of professional boundaries and their professional role. They need to be able to identify and analyse instances when their own needs may influence their responses and take action to address this. For example, students may be visiting households where the emotional or physical needs of children are not met. While it may be tempting to try and bridge the gap or personally compensate, this might mean that students cross professional boundaries and they need to be able to reflect critically on their own motives and the needs of children. From consultation with a service user representative, it was clear that children and young people valued dedicated workers who actually cared about what happened to them. In being clear about their boundaries we do not want students to lose this personal commitment to individuals. Whilst at university and on practice learning opportunities, students should be encouraged to explore personal/professional boundaries using case scenarios. Some of these scenarios should draw on child care and protection. Social workers have a range of powers and responsibilities underpinned by legal frameworks and relevant guidance. Students need to develop the confidence to use their authority appropriately. Within child care and protection they need to be able to balance their duties to protect children with their responsibilities not to intervene unnecessarily. Here students would be expected to demonstrate (through supervision, tutorials, role play and written work) that they can evidence the basis for any decision using research, appropriate assessment tools and analysis.	*Autonomy* - Deal with complex ethical and professional issues in accordance with current professional and/or ethical codes of practice. *Autonomy* - exercise autonomy and initiative in professional/equivalent activities. *Cognitive* - Demonstrate some originality and creativity in dealing with professional level issues. *Practice* - practise in a range of professional level contexts which includes a degree of unpredictability and/or specialism. *Knowledge* - detailed knowledge and understanding in one or more specialisms.	Understanding and managing complex ethical issues: - Act appropriately, even in uncertain and ambiguous circumstances and critically reflect on and learn from the outcomes. Working within agreed standards of social work practice: - Critically reflect on their practice and performance and modify these as a result. Managing, presenting and sharing records and reports: - Provide clear evidence for judgments and decisions.

58

	POST-GRADUATE ROUTE	SCQF Level 10	Standards in Social Work Education
Professional Confidence and Competence	Students need to demonstrate that they can exercise initiative and work autonomously. However, they also need to demonstrate that they will seek appropriate support and guidance through supervision and that they are clear as to the value and purpose of supervision. In particular they need to be clear about the role of supervision on the decision making process. Students should be equipped to expect a quality of supervision that will enable them to discuss complex and 'grey' areas of concern about a child's wellbeing. Students should expect that one of the purposes of supervision is to have their assessments challenged.	*Autonomy* - exercise autonomy and initiative in professional/equivalent activities. *Autonomy* - Work effectively under guidance in a peer relationship with qualified practitioners.	Managing one's own work in an accountable way: - Use professional and managerial supervision and support to improve their practice.
	Students need to be competent and confident at translating their knowledge of risk assessment in to practice in child care and protection. This is reflected in the 21st Century Social Work Review Interim Report (2005) which states that social workers "need to be able to make complex decisions about the level of risk. This requires a high level of skill and personal autonomy and accountability".	*Knowledge* - detailed knowledge and understanding in one or more specialisms.	Assessing and managing risks: - Identify, assess and record the nature of risk, its seriousness and the harm that is may cause.

	POST-GRADUATE ROUTE	SCQF Level 10	Standards in Social Work Education
Professional Confidence and Competence	Children and young people may not be in a position to articulate their own needs. They require social workers who are skilled and confident at accurately communicating in a range of formal and informal settings. Social workers who are unable to do this verbally and in writing will do children a disservice. The Executive Recommendations and summary from the Inquiry into the death of Caleb Ness criticised the report prepared for the case conference. It stated that "the report was inaccurate in vital respects. It suggested that the couple were stable whereas in fact Shirley had made Alec move out a few weeks previously. The gaps in information relating to the two older children in care, Alec's brain injury, the nature and extent of the criminal records of both parents were not identified. The child protection case conference was not told that Caleb was suffering from neo natal abstinence syndrome" (O'Brien, 2003, 7).

A student's ability to communicate effectively can be assessed in the HEI through role playing case conferences, Children's Hearings and in practice learning opportunities by presenting their own assessments to similar forums. For example, a student undertaking their practice learning opportunity within adult services might be asked to present their assessment of parenting capacity to a multi-agency group. | *Communication* - make formal presentations about specialised topics.

Communication - communicate with professional level peers etc.

Cognitive - make judgments where information is limited or comes from a range of sources. | Preparing for and taking part in decision making forums:
- Present evidence to decision making forums and help individuals, families etc to understand the procedures involved and the possible and actual outcomes.

Working within agreed standards of social work practice:
- Use appropriate assertiveness in justifying professional decisions and upholding social work practice values. |

	POST-GRADUATE ROUTE	SCQF Level 10	Standards in Social Work Education
Values and Ethical Practice	Students must demonstrate ethical practice based on SSSC Codes of Practice, 2003. The 21st Century Review Report 'Changing Lives' states that "Social work is based on respect for the inherent worth and dignity of all people and the rights that flow from this..." (2006). Students will be expected to read this and other key documents and to consider how they apply to children and young people.	*Knowledge* - knowledge that covers and integrates most of the principal areas of the subject.	Working within agreed standards of social work practice: - Work at all times within the professional codes of practice, ethical principles and service standards that underpin high quality social work practice.
	Students need to demonstrate that they are aware of their own personal values in relation to child care and protection. In accordance with Standards in Social work education, students should demonstrate that they can overcome personal prejudices to respond appropriately to identified need. For example, a student might be asked to reflect on their feelings about supervising contact between a registered sex offender and his/her child. Students should expect to be challenged if they express views which are in conflict with social work values. The focus of this is that as practitioners they will need to be able to provide a professional service to a range of service users whose circumstances, behaviour or views may challenge their value base. This might include adults, children and young people who exhibit sexually harmful behaviour, asylum seekers and their children, substance misusing parents.	*Knowledge* - a critical understanding of the principal theories/concepts and principles.	Understanding and managing complex ethical issues: - Identify, understand and critically evaluate ethical issues, dilemmas and conflicts affecting their practice.

61

	POST-GRADUATE ROUTE	SCQF Level 10	Standards in Social Work Education
Values and Ethical Practice	Students are expected to demonstrate a readiness to reflect on their own values and experiences and consider the impact these may have on their assessment and intervention generally. Specific to child care and protection, they will be expected to start to consider the relevance of their own attachment experiences/experience of parenting to their future practice. For example, students should be asked to reflect on their own experience and views of discipline and how these may influence their practice in the context of current legal frameworks.	*Autonomy* - deal with complex ethical and professional issues in accordance with current professional and/or codes of practice.	Understanding and managing complex ethical issues: - Devise effective strategies to deal with ethical issues, dilemmas and conflicts. Working within agreed standards of social work practice: - Critically reflect on their practice and performance and modify these as a result.
	Students need to demonstrate that where there is a conflict between their personal and professional values, they can use supervision effectively to address this.	*Autonomy* - work effectively under guidance in a peer relationship with qualified practitioners. *Autonomy* - work with others to bring about change, development and/or new thinking.	Managing one's own work in an accountable way: - Use professional and managerial supervision and support to improve their practice. Promoting best social work practice: - Use supervision together with other organisational and professional systems to influence courses of action where practice falls below the standards required.

	POST-GRADUATE ROUTE	SCQF Level 10	Standards in Social Work Education
Values and Ethical Practice	Most HEIs have developed links with service users and carers and they should have some input into the student's early learning opportunities. We recommend that one of the areas explored is how service users have experienced social work intervention. As it may be difficult for children and parents currently involved in the child protection system to speak about their experiences, HEIs may need to employ other resources (video, DVD, audio tape) to ensure that this group is represented. Morris and Smith developed and evaluated a video of mothers talking about their experiences of investigations. They found that one of the factors which prevented women participating was the anxiety that they would be judged by the viewer (NCH, 1995).	*Knowledge* - a critical understanding of the principal theories, concepts and principles. *Cognitive* - critically identify, define, conceptualise and analyse complex professional level problems and issues.	Assessing needs and options in order to recommend a course of action: - Listen actively to people who use services and their carers, respecting their experience and taking full account of their views. Working within agreed standards of social work practice: - Work at all times within the professional codes of practice, ethical principles and service standards that underpin high quality social work practice.
	In accordance with SSSC Codes of Practice (2003) students must promote equal opportunities and respect diversity, treating all people with dignity and respect. Students will be expected to show that they can demonstrate social work values in their relationships with their peers and teaching staff as well as service users and carers. Students who cannot treat their fellow students with dignity and respect should not have access to service users and carers and may not be able to progress with their studies.	*Autonomy* - practise in ways which show a clear awareness of own and others' roles and responsibilities.	Working effectively with professionals: - Deal constructively with disagreements and conflict within work relationships.

Values and Ethical Practice	POST-GRADUATE ROUTE	SCQF Level 10	Standards in Social Work Education
	Students need to demonstrate that they are aware of the impact of discrimination on service users and have taken responsibility to challenge this in an appropriate way. With reference to child care and protection, students need to demonstrate that they are aware of how children can be discriminated against and how this can add to their vulnerability.

There may be some children who are more vulnerable than others. For example Kennedy states "large numbers of disabled children use an alternative form of communication and a range of methods to communicate" (in Wilson and James, 2004, 152) and practitioners did not have the skills to communicate. Students need to show they are aware of their responsibility to access additional support services. | *Knowledge* - detailed knowledge and understanding in one or more specialisms.

Practice - use a few skills which are specialised. | Understanding and managing complex ethical issues:
- Identify, understand and critically evaluate ethical issues, dilemmas and conflicts affecting their practice.

Understanding and managing complex ethical issues:
- Devise effective strategies to deal with ethical issues, dilemmas and conflicts. |
| | Students need to be aware that their professional assessment of a child's needs may be in conflict with that of the agency. For example, there may be instances when the decision to provide or withdraw services is based on resources rather than need. Students need to demonstrate an ability to challenge appropriately to ensure that they discharge their professional responsibility. | *Autonomy* - exercise autonomy and initiative in professional/equivalent activities.

Cognitive - offer professional level insights, interpretations and solutions to problems and issues.

Communication - communicate with professional level peers, seniors etc. | Promoting best social work practice:
- Use supervision, together with other organisational and professional systems to influence courses of action where practice falls below the standards required.

Working within agreed standards of social work practice:
- Use appropriate assertiveness in justifying professional decisions and upholding social work practice values. |

	POST-GRADUATE ROUTE	SCQF Level 10	Standards in Social Work Education
Values and Ethical Practice	While discharging their authority students may encounter aggression or abuse from service users. Students need to demonstrate that they can seek appropriate supervision to ensure that their professional assessment and intervention is not compromised. Students need to be clear that it is not acceptable to carry out their duties in an unsafe environment. Being aware of their own safety does not mean that students abrogate their responsibility for the well being of service users. For example, if a student assesses that it is not safe for him/her to enter a house to visit a child because s/he hears an argument, s/he needs to be aware of the impact this could be having on the child's welfare and take appropriate and timely action. This could include referral to another agency eg the police.	*Practice* - practise in a range of professional contexts which include a degree of unpredictability and/or specialism. *Cognitive* - make judgements where information is limited or comes from a range of skills.	Understanding and managing complex ethical issues: - Act appropriately, even in uncertain and ambiguous circumstances and critically reflect on and learn from the outcomes. Assessing and managing risk: - Assess, analyse and record potential risk to themselves and colleagues.
	Students should be aware of the outcomes of their intervention including unintended outcomes. For example, while it may support parents with learning difficulties to provide extensive home care, this may have the unintended outcome of increasing their child's vulnerability and attachment difficulties.	*Knowledge* - A critical understanding of the principal theories, concepts and principles *Practice* - practise in a range of professional level contexts which include a degree of unpredictability and/or specialism *Autonomy* - Deal with complex ethical and professional issues in accordance with current professional and/or ethical codes of practice	Working within agreed standards of social work practice: - Critically reflect on their practice and performance and modify these as a result. Assessing and managing risk: - Plan, monitor, review and record outcomes and actions taken to minimise risk, stress and harm. Assessing and managing risk: - Review intentions and actions in the light of expected and unintended consequences.

Bibliography:

Antisocial Behaviour etc. (Scotland) Act 2004, Crown Copyright

Black, A and Burgham, A (2003) *Child Review Report into the Life and Death of Carla Nicole Bone,* North East of Scotland Child Protection Committee

Butler-Sloss, E (1987) *Report of the Inquiry into Child Abuse in Cleveland 1989*, London, HMSO

Children (Scotland) Act 1995, Crown Copyright

Clyde, Lord (1992) *Inquiry into the Removal of Children from Orkney in February 1991*, Edinburgh, HMSO

Department for Education and Skills (2005) *Common Core of Skills and Knowledge for the Children's Workforce*

Department of Health (2000) *Framework for the Assessment of Children in Need and their Families*

Department of Health (2001) *Studies informing Framework for the Assessment of Children in Need and their Families,* London, The Stationery Office

Department of Health (2004) *The Ten Essential Shared Capabilities: A Framework for the Whole of the Mental Health Workforce*

Department of Health & Social Security (1974) *Report of the Committee of Inquiry into the Care and Supervision Provided in Relation to Maria Colwell*

Fostering of Children (Scotland) Regulations 1996, Crown Copyright

Horwath, J and Shardlow, S (2003) *Making links across specialisms: understanding modern social work practice,* Lyme Regis, Russell House

Howe, D (1987) *An Introduction to Social Work Theory,* Aldershot, Gower

Knapman, J and Morrison, T (2005) *Making the Most of Supervision in Health and Social Care,* Brighton, Pavilion

Laming, Lord (2003), The *Victoria Climbie Inquiry*, Report presented to Parliament by the Secretary of State for Health and the Secretary of State for the Home Office, London, The Stationery Office

MacDonald, G and Winkley, A (2000) *What Works in Child Protection? - Summary*, Barnardos, Essex

Mental Health (Care and Treatment) (Scotland) Act 2003, Crown Copyright

Morris K, and Smith K (1995) *Child Protection Enquiries: Mothers Talk about their experiences,* NCH Action for Children, Family Rights Group, London

O'Brien, S (2003) *Report of the Caleb Ness Inquiry,* Edinburgh, Edinburgh and the Lothians Child Protection Committee

Reder, P; Duncan, S and Gray, M, (1993) *Beyond Blame Child Abuse Tragedies Revisited,* Routledge, London

Reder, P and Duncan, S (2004) 'Making the Most of the Victoria Climbie report', *Child Abuse Review,* Vol 13, 95-114

Scottish Credit and Qualifications Framework (2003) *An Introduction to the Scottish Credit and Qualifications Framework 2nd Edition*

Scottish Executive (2002) "It's Everyone's Job to Make Sure I'm Alright" *Report of the Child Protection Audit and Review*, Edinburgh, Scottish Executive

Scottish Executive (2003) *Framework for Social Work Education in Scotland: Standards in Social Work Education*, Edinburgh, Scottish Executive

Scottish Executive (2003) *Getting Our Priorities Right: Good Practice Guidance for Working with Children and Families affected by Substance Misuse,* Edinburgh, Scottish Executive

Scottish Executive (2004) *Protecting Children and Young People: Framework for Standards,* Edinburgh, Scottish Executive

Scottish Executive (2004) *Protecting Children and Young People: The Charter,* Edinburgh, Scottish Executive

Scottish Executive (2005) *Getting it Right for Every Child - Consultation Document,* Edinburgh, Scottish Executive

Scottish Executive (2005) *21st Century Review of Social Work - Interim Report,* Edinburgh, Scottish Executive

Scottish Executive (2006) *21st Century Review – Changing Lives*, Edinburgh, Scottish Executive

Scottish Office (1998) *Protecting Children – A Shared Responsibility: Guidance on Interagency Cooperation,* Edinburgh, HMSO

Scottish Office (1999) *Looking after Children in Scotland: Good Parenting, Good Outcomes,* Edinburgh, The Scottish Office

Scottish Practice Learning Project (2006) *Standards and audit for practice learning opportunities: A quality process,* Dundee, Scottish Practice Learning Project

Scottish Social Services Council (2003) *Codes of Practice for Social Service Workers and Employers*, Dundee, Scottish Social Services Council

Scottish Social Services Council (2003) *Registration Rules,* Dundee, Scottish Social Services Council

Social Work Inspection Agency (2005) *An Inspection into the Care and Protection of Children in Eilean Siar,* Edinburgh, Scottish Executive

United Nations (1989) Convention on the Rights of the Child

Walker, AG (2005), *Introduction to handout selection – revised February 2003,* University of Dundee Conference: Investigative Interviewing of Children

Wilson, K and James. A, (2004) *Child Protection Handbook, 2nd Edition,* London, Balliere Tindall

Consultation Process

Organisations and individuals who were consulted during the development of KCs:

- Aberlour, Linda Grierson

- Association of Directors of Social Work, Child Protection Sub Group

- Dundee Voluntary Action, Stuart Eno

- Glasgow Caledonian University, Jo Burns

- Glasgow School of Social Work, Pam Green Lister

- Open University, Sue Dumbleton

- Representatives from the Federation of Funded Practice Teaching Units

- Representatives at the Scottish Practice Learning Project Meeting for Practice Learning Co-ordinators

- Robert Gordon University, Robert Buckley

- Robert Gordon University, Stewart Brodie

- Scottish Executive, Child Protection Reform Programme Team, Tim Warren

- Scottish Practice Learning Project, Cathy Macnaughton

- Scottish Social Services Council, Ama Okoh

- Scottish Social Services Council, Brian Smith

- Students undertaking the Supervision and Training Module at Dundee University

- Students undertaking the Introduction to Child Care and Protection at Dundee University

- University of Dundee, Di Part

- University of Edinburgh, Gary Clapton

- University of Paisley, Clare Devine

- University of Stirling, Jacqui Casher

- University of Stirling, Rona Woodward

- Who Cares Scotland, Deirdre Watson

The Child Protection Training and Development Project was funded by the Scottish Executive and commissioned to the Scottish Institute for Excellence in Social Work Education. It was completed between 2004-2006 using a collaborative approach, with project staff working closely with academics and practitioners from across Scotland. (see Appendix 1)

Project staff were drawn from the University of Dundee Child Protection Unit led by Professor Brigid Daniel with overall project management resting with the Institute.

Project Lead:
Professor Brigid Daniel

Project Manager:
Linda Walker

Project Officers:
Helen Whincup
Margaret Bruce